THE
GTFO
POETRY
JOURNAL
2024

First Edition, October 2024

©2024 GTFO POETRY

ISBN: 9798340183118

Cover Image by Kay Miller

Edited by Anthony Xavier Jackson
and Kay Miller

Table of Contents.

Introduction
Dedication/ Acknowledgement

Introduction

GTFO was founded by an ongoing conversation which arose after the sale of Luna's café. Naturally, a marked absence of venue was visited upon all the poets and performers who had so long counted on Jose Montoya's Poetry Unplugged Series on Thursday nights, and we wanted to do something about that, we wanted to make sure the void could be filled with community, poetry, connection and all the beauty that was nurtured by Art Luna with his business.

It is in this vein, that this journal was proposed and realized, a sort of giant open mic on paper for the beloved poets of our town whose voices have been there since the demise of Luna's but have perhaps not been given a venue as consistent as Luna's.

Below you will find a quote from each of the GTFO members regarding the community and this project. We hope this will suffice as an introduction to who we are and what we do.

****

Anthony: I have been extremely honored to be the editor of this project. I know many of the people in this volume from readings but have gained new insight into them by reading and selecting their poems. Sacramento has been my home as an artist for a few years now, and has welcomed me with open arms. Community is when a conversation between acts, in alleys, over mota and cigarettes becomes a reality that looks like podcasts, field interviews, theatrical presentations and cross pollination with other writers and groups.

AL: This community has been there for me on the days and nights when I wasn't sure I could be there for myself. Thank you so much for coming on this journal with us.

Tony: Thank you to every poet who submitted and anyone reading this. The Genesis for the GTFO journal occurred while slamming beers in the alley next to Luna's Cafe with Kay Miller. I mentioned the WTF journal the late Frank Andrick (former Luna's host) would publish featuring local poets. We both agreed that it could be something. GTFO's journal is the embodiment of our collective's goal. The showcasing of the diversity of our local poets and the various open mics being established in the aftermath of Covid. GTFO encourages, supports and celebrates our community with recognition and opportunities to come together through poetry.

Kay: This journal took a whole lot of work and energy by some amazing people to see the light of your living room. But dive down into it and you'll see the very lifeblood of the creative scene in Sacramento is right here in this collection. For that reason, I humbly offer what little I can do for this amazing city and community. Thank you to everyone who submitted, to anyone who ever gave a shit about us, and to my friends and co-poets in the GTFO collective. Go GTFOrce! And remember, don't be an asshole

This journal is dedicated to the Sacramento Poetry Community.

Acknowledgments

First and foremost, we would like to acknowledge Art Luna for supporting the poetry scene in Sacramento with the longest running open mic in California, Jose Montoya's Poetry Unplugged.
We would like to thank Patrick Grizzell of Sacramento Poetry Center for his gracious and generous support of this, the first of what we hope will become many annual journals of Sacramento's poetry voices.
We would also like to thank the Sacramento Poet Laureate, Andru Defeye for granting us an awesome back cover quote and always working tirelessly to support the community at large with spectacular events such as Sacramento Poetry Week.
Finally, we would like to thank you who have stepped into this space with us and supported these poets.

GTFO

WTF is it?
Is it
Gorgeously Telling Folklore Oracles?
Parables spun through lucid lips
splattered with spirit when the tale is told with
Fables
Poems
Cautionary Tales are gifts
A stew now simmering from an imagination that is lit
Is it I'm
Gonna Tryta Fight Oligarchs
in my own tongue?
What if puns are guns
that heal open broken wounds?
What pains you pales within
the glow of a mama's lullaby
So I won't be shy tattling on lies
pushed by profiteer's proclivity to
pilfer retirement pensions
Gouging & grabbing for greed
even though they have not the need
Is it
Gravitational Tides Fill Oceans?
Swelling swollen bodies of
saltwater saints & seaweeds
Leviathans
Krakens
Entranced Creatures
Below-the-Bottom Feeders
of the darkest deepest depths
percolating to the surface
to gamble in shaken shell games
and bruising battles of Goliaths
Is it
Gargantuan Titans Fighting Obsessively?

Kaiju cracking mantles
The cacophony calamity causes

like crushing fists of Kongs
Hydras healing their hewn heads
Cryptids livid in the legends
given by Living Gods
Is it
Gods Tread Forward Omnisciently?
Tip-toeing & stomping
on a whim &
a storm &
a penitent prayer
lifted to their nostrils through incessant incense smoke
Inhaled with serenading serenity
or tumultuous terror
The rearing of bipolar caps
answer the litanies
Emitting/absorbing
the ruptured rapture of wrath &
benign benevolent blessings
for us fledgling fleshlings...
Is it
Groping 'Til Fungi Overcome
our feeble senses?
Unwholy humans
humming on fumes
Smashing squashing green things
Not looking when sprinting
full speed on speed
towards the cliff's lip
Diving into dangers of a darkened heart
not knowing where they're going
With NO plan
Until BLAM! or
BOOM! or
SPLAT! or

ACK! or
AHHH! or
OH SH!T! or
SQUISH!
Is it
Going To Feel Orgasmic?

Undulating & squishy
Pungent & sticky
licking that icky
Moaning & jonesing
Wailing while writhing
Riding while crying
Trusting while thrusting
Scratching the deep itch in the ditch
Saturating that pole with inner soul
Whispering while dripping
Lusting & kissing
Loving & missing
Missing you already
Yet again, I'm ready...
And again,
WTF is
GTFO?
It's the ways we
Get
To
Finish
Ourselves…

*Mario Ellis Hill began writing & performing poetry in the early
1990's, and has since made an impact as a featured
poet/spoken word artist throughout the Sacramento region,
California, and beyond. He is the founder & leader of the Mario
Ellis Hill Poetry Machine - a performance group of rotating
artists that fuses spoken word, live music, movement & song.*

Mario served as a co-host of Joe Montoya's Poetry Unplugged! Open Mic Series in Sacramento, CA, and host of Open Stage Open Mic Series in Davis, CA. Besides featuring at poetry venues & open mics, Mario also delved into the world of slam.

Advice for 2050

Advice for the United World Government in 2050

Ask politely if the companies making can openers will crack open Yellowstone (you can't feed everyone.)

Throw big parties for the citizens who follow the rules.

(Rule number one: All parties not sanctioned by the State are restricted to gatherings of no more than six persons and are required to apply for a party permit through DOGSAP, the Department of Gathering, Speech and Press. This includes parties taking place at private residences. Alcohol is strictly prohibited. Persons found guilty of partying without the proper permits, or of partying outside of these restrictions will be subject to prosecution under the terms of the Anti-Sedition Act of 2038.)

Purchase FIFA and enlist the athletes as a new branch of the military.

Take Mark Ruffalo and run him unopposed for emperor of the known universe (should still be alive for a hot minute with your medical technology.) But don't give him any power and don't tell him we don't know shit about the known universe.

The proletariat wants reparations. Pay them in lip service concerning god and glitter.

Illegalize excessive cat ownership.

Socialize opioids.

Redesign the flag every couple years so's we don't get bored.

Don't skimp on the state-sponsored orgies.

Advice for the Peasant in 2050

Don't believe in God or glitter (there is no god and fuck glitter.)

Party. Party. Party.

Pledge allegiance to the rainbow and a geometry book.

Farm some chicken and zucchini. The robots do all the other work, anyway.

Try not to breed if you are bad at soccer. (At least try.)

Remove your state-implanted tracking antenna and replace it with a Twizzler. The same company makes the both of them by roughly the same specifications and it's better to attract squirrels than the IRS's SWAT team.

Government drugs are better than what you can buy off the street.

Own one, maybe two cats. No more!

If you are invited to an orgy, just go. Nothing that bad has ever happened at an orgy.

Vote Mark Ruffalo for emperor.

Kory Vance is a poet, fiction writer, affordable housing professional, and amateur strongman living in Sacramento, California. He is the author of the speculative poetry volume, Poems About Aliens. In his poems, Kory employs soft world-building techniques to immerse his readers in a world of poetry. His work can be found in The Oakland Review, The Antonym:

Bridge to Global Literature, Salmon Creek Journal, Sinking City Southern Florida Poetry Journal, and more. Kory is currently seeking publication for his first novel while writing his second, as well as working on two new volumes of poetry titled Bury me with Rosemary and Animals Drinking Beer. Follow Kory's work on Instagram: @strength_and_poetry.

Poetry

if your chicken's sick
get two milk crates, solid plastic
two bungee cords
attach one milk crate to your rear-mounted bike rack with the
first bungee cord
put the chicken in the first milk crate
and set the other one (face up) on top
the inner rim will let it seat on top of the first securely
loop the second bungee cord through the handles of the second
milk crate
pump your tires
wear your helmet
remember a bottle of water because it's 99 degrees out
the exotic vet is straight down that road

*Kyle Griffiths is a resident of the Sacramento area and works for
the state of California. He holds a Master of Fine Arts in
Creative Inquiry from the California Institute of Integral Studies.
As an interdisciplinary artist he has exhibited visual art and
created performances in San Francisco and the Sacramento
area.*

Culture

Kept in the songs
Sang at the top of lungs
in the dead of night
lifting spirits

dripping from brushes
coloring outside of lines
they have told us were limits

recipes that remind us of home
heal broken hearts

fashion that fits like we feel on the inside

prayers passed down from our ancestors
smuggled across borders in our bloodstreams

something sacred to be safeguarded as such.

Sacramento is still finding its culture
Somewhere between Sutter and Stephon Clark
the arc of our story
accountable to our past
prejudice still prevalent in the foundation beneath our feet
must be mended
can't remain cracked
for our children to slip through
Did you
know that Jedediah Smith was a slave owner
native killer
when you
paved that path through the city with his name on it….
Where are we trying to get to?
We talk Gold but not enough
about the people that were crushed

It was a stampede not a rush
that we still celebrate
reading land acknowledgements
dancing on Maidu graves
afraid to read that chapter outloud
but still trying to turn the page

and maybe that's part of why my city is in crisis over its identity

Currently
waves
of weary wandering
wash up on our streets
communities built under bridges to keep
walled from weather either hiding from heat
or literally left out in the cold
Same time we are sold
stories that say our team is finally winning
and I wonder if we shouldn't be shooting our light
to the people on the ground instead of at the sky
I wonder why my city clips the wings of those we learn to fly
from
by nullifying nests they rest their heads in
What is world class cuisine unless everyone has a plate
or a mural fest if the artists aren't getting paid?

Don't get the wrong idea.
I love my city.
I just don't paint pretty pictures
over rough realities without priming
because as any artists knows
that's how you get bleed through
Sacramento, I see you

When kidnapped immigrants show up on our doorstep
and are welcomed with open arms and opportunities I see you.
When a pandemic hits and residents are replenished
by love in local restaurants, I see you.

That's my city.

The one where we frontline against fascism
address people by proper pronouns
fly rainbows over city hall
and shut down arenas
because human rights are not a game
and they'll never matter more than one

The way we cultivate community
because compassion is not a commodity
construct altars as part of our protests
revitalize with radical joy

Sacramento your youth are speaking you into existence and
We just need to listen

Picture

Business owners, artists, and politicians
at the same table
talking transformation
trusting truth to lead the conversation
Honesty and patience with one another
with no other
just us
talking justice
knowing what is
isn't what has to be just because it's always been

Picture incubation
of innovation
Soaring without fearing the fall
Building with not for
Involving us all

Equity at every interaction
Diversity leading every dialog
Inclusion in every undertaking

Manifest

More than middle of the road
Give 'em gold bridges
from vision to fruition
that's what this is.

Sacramento. Culture.
Is kept by the creatives
curated by conviction
Kept alive by our commitment

to moments like this
Our city, a renaissance ready for its unfolding
can you feel it?

THATS HOW CULTURE GETS CREATED.

Whether sharing stages with legendary beat poets or your favorite Hip Hop emcees, Andru Defeye's unorthodox writing and performance style has made him a fixture behind microphones around the country. 2020 saw the release of his critically acclaimed Frequency album followed shortly after by his crowning as the youngest Poet Laureate in California capitol history. In 2021, Defeye was listed by Sacramento Magazine as one of the city's 100 business leaders and nominated to receive an honorary doctorate from CSUS. In 2022 he joined the ranks of some of the most celebrated poets in the country as an Academy of American Poets fellow and brought Sacramento Poetry Day (October 26th) to life creating a locally sourced curriculum, collection, and contest and bringing it to over

250,000 youth in the Sacramento area. In 2023 these efforts earned him a key to the city. From Sacramento to Staten Island and SXSW, Andru Defeye

It's 930PM on a Tuesday and I'm trying to remember a password

There is such a thing as
wine from
dandelions
Crushed buds
turning water yellow and cloudy

It's how I'm
courting bitterness
Sipping mashed leaves
and poisons
Sitting at a desk
Flattop sleek
and marred by
detritus of felled trees
and the wet shadow
of a half full glass
A sticky note on the
bottom of the monitor
in your handwriting like
cars going too fast
on crowded freeways
It says

I hope you find your peace

I'm shaking again
but slowly
It's just me with thoughts
of flesh and absence

and candle wicks surrounded
by puddles of soy
It's me and fermented dandelions
Dragging cursor to
the bottom of the login in
screen and pointedly
filling the
box

Remember me

Kay Miller, a narrative poet from Sacramento, has been captivating audiences with their poetry for decades. Their work offers a raw glimpse into the America in Sacramento, seen through liquor store windows and dirty car mirrors. With brutal honesty, they navigate the urban landscape, shedding light on both its struggles and moments of beauty. Kay's art serves as a powerful reminder of the resilience of the human spirit and the importance of LGBTQA+ perspectives in poetry. Kay is a founding member of the GTFO Poetry Collective.

Happy Father's Day

She

was to be

his princess

dark blue suit

light pink dress

screaming or smiling

her grimace is graceful

how did you forget to love her?

to blink your eyes with her in mind?

you are unfit

full of lumps of brown stuff at the dog park

how could you be so heartless

and leave her

in a world full of people

who only want to take her in parts

You could have been her whole

she has trouble expecting the world to do something that not even you would do

embrace her

because like them

You pretend not to know her

how do you think it makes her feel?

I hope you feel lousy

you're a coward

and you owe me dresses

lots of dresses

One for every dance I missed

Because it wasn't meant

for mommy to be my partner

the ticket admitted permission for two

a daddy

and a daughter

and there I was

your dress-less

daddy-less daughter

what about school?

what about donuts with dad?

shopping for new shoes and plaid?

dad you never showed up to take me

I had forgiven you then

but as for lately

I have bigger concerns

like explaining to my young

how a person can both be alive yet dead

yes, dead

Because parts of you stop living

when you left me

I am your child

I know you didn't really forget me

maybe you meant to love me

but couldn't figure it out

had you waited to see my smile

I am certain that you have filled out your doubts

you should have been waiting at the end of the terminal for me

To pick up my bags and whatever else I would need

but selfishly

you put your own desires first

and now I have to pack up my feelings

and send them off in a hearse

I am going to bury his ashes in your front yard

the emotions of your child

she had to discard

because you never even sent a card to acknowledge her birth

daddy, I have had 36 of them

I am done waiting

it is apparent

you are not coming back

to fill in what I lack

to help me pack my backpack

do my homework

or paint stories of my dreams

I have managed to live without you

but things are not as great as they seem

this poem speaks my heart

along with other countless things

my unfulfilled reality

the vitality in my existence

my determination to be the best woman I can be without you

and I am coming with a vengeance

because although I have missed you

I am pissed too

it's been more than 36 years

 and I am still trying to forget you

a man who's voice this poet has never heard

I surely hope you find shame in your mistake

Life has offered you countless years

yet here we are at your wake

Consider this your eulogy papa

with these words

you have been laid to rest

because I am no longer making room for you

but I am sending you my best

signed

your dress-less

daddy-less daughter

Shewrights is a curious, courageous, and strategic thinker. She dabbles in several forms of self-expression. She refers to her genre of art as Artivism. Artivism= Art+Activism. She writes for self-care, creativity, and clarity. She shares to connect with others who love and value self-expression.

Revel

I take intense pleasure or satisfaction
In being alone.
There's a sense of safety being me,
Whether I'm out or I'm home.

I revel in the fact that life is,
In the fact that God loves me,
In the fact that I can simply live
I revel in the fact that I can be.

Sometimes people exhaust me.
It's crazy to think how vain & empty we are,
How we're so absorbed in ourselves,
And how from that thought, I'm not very far.

So sometimes I like to be alone,
To go to the movies by myself,
Maybe a coffee shop or a restaurant,
Or buying things to fill up my bookshelf.

I ponder my lameness, and others greatness
How I don't have the motivation,
How my dreams will never be reached,
And I blame my lack of volition.

But I still like being alone
There's no one to impress
No one to bore
No one to stress.

I can think and ponder
I can write as many poems as I want,
And no one can judge them,
Or make fun or taunt.

When I'm by-myself it's just me

And no one else,
There's no one to compare too
No one to stand against.

I can ponder philosophy
And have debates in head
And I can win all of the arguments.
I can be silly, Dance and not go to bed

I don't have to bend who I am,
To fit those around me.
I don't have to play pretend,
Because I know who they want me to be

So, I am satisfied being alone
And I won't be lonely.
I take pleasure in being myself, completely.
I can exit, purely and simply.

Valeriya Timoshenko calls herself a wanna be poet. She's an English major at sac state and hopes to one day be an English teacher that works in schools that need extra love. She loves to read and write, loves hiking and traveling, and loves to watch people live out life.

Company

There will be company again someday
Strangers' hands behind my knees
The scent of you and YSL Libre won't haunt me

Tonight though, it follows me home
Hangs in my closet
Drapes an arm lazily across my chest
Trails polished iridescent lavender fingernails individually down
the rungs of my ribcage
Unwinds itself and slips out the door before morning

I catch myself searching for her (your scent)
Behind the books I never read you
In the background of the TV shows we didn't finish
In the clothing of mine you wore
In the clothing of yours I still wear
Under every sticker backing I peel off
She lives eternal in the crack under my bedroom door
A pet I locked out to sleep easier

*Diana Rose Winter is a writer and cinnamon roll aficionado
based in her hometown of Sacramento, CA. She has been
either writing or avoiding writing her whole life, and frequenting
poetry open mic nights since February of 2023. When not busy
with the demanding day job of existing while disabled, she is
sinking her teeth into all things local, and can most likely be
found purchasing unnecessary additional butterfly hair clips.*

Hubris

He extracts wax and honey from a honeybee hive.
His busyness a boondoggle; enough of a distraction.
His thick armor, not enough.
He gets stung on his ankle above the heal
and it begins to swell immediately.
With a limp now, he collects feathers from his chickens
and the owl that would not allow him to sleep,
hooting in the night, heckling him as he hunched
in the shadows. He collects the feathers strewn
from all the birds hunting in the labyrinth
of his home: so many walls of cactus.
He uses these items to construct his own wings.
He wants to fly high and perch himself above all else.
I warned him that I am the sun;
he is the moon, waxing and waning, dark
unless I shine upon him.
He did not believe me.
But now, he comes too close
with waxen wings, thinking he will
put me in his pocket along with the honey,
to be taken out on a whim or when hunger hits.
Instead, he is evaporated by my heat, now nothing
but hot wind blowing upcanyon in the afternoon.
I no longer have to shout his name
into the wind, I merely have to whisper.

*Maria Steinhauser is a middle school ELA/History teacher in the
Sacramento area and has a Creative Writing MFA in poetry.
She finds her inspiration running the trails of Northern California
and spending time in nature.*

Skin Deep

When talking about my culture,
I am often met with the question
What are you
As though there is an otherness to me
I am something foreign
Something not connected to their humanness

I was once told not to worry, because I don't look Mexican

As long as I don't "look" Mexican then I can be accepted
As though looking Mexican somehow brought Shame?
As though Being Mexican was something to hide?

As though my Mexican, my indigenous blood
Was something that only ran skin deep
That the look of me was all that mattered
All that translated from their eyes to the mind to the heart

That the women who came before me didn't exist

My great Abuelas fear crossing the invisible border in the night,

Remaining invisible
till she learned English
yet still viewed as
in between
in her humanness

she never was

That My Nonnie didn't translate school projects
for her undocumented classmates
Who Was a strong willed Chicana
despite the leer
Of white washed eyes

The way my mother rolls tortillas, t
hat to me taste like home

These women, my ancestors
their dark tan skin, warm from
Mexico's Summer sun
all but forgotten, not note-able

That there is a shallowness to my nature, that all that
One sees is what's reflected in my face

If that's the case
Let me bath under the sun, heat, the yellow
Glinty rays
Until My skin
so shimmering bronze
Will blind the racism
from your eyes

Rina Wakefield is a Spoken Word Performer, writer, Podcast Producer, Poetry/Storytelling event Producer/Host, Women's Rights & Arts Activist, and member of Myrtle Tree Arts from Northern California. She is a Master's Degree candidate studying Library Science with a focus on Rare Book Curation and Archives from San Jose State University. She holds a Bachelor of Arts Degree in English Literature from Sacramento State University.
She is currently working on a prose poetry chapbook, as well as a creative non-fiction novel based on the female lineage of her Indigenous and Native American heritage. Her family line comes from the Purepecha people of the northwestern region of Michoacán, Mexico.

The Smile

This smile you see I made that

I took the pain and trauma of my childhood and made rainbows out of the rain

The determination you see I made that

I took the failed attempts of the elders who raised me and decided to recreate the path that saved me

The peace you see I made that I took the bullets of a gloc and raced the clock to create my own time to shine

The vibe you feel I made that

I took the chaos and made community

I took the anxiety and made love

The change you see I made that

I made that

I made that

I made me

LifeofLaura has been writing 17 years in secret. In 2022 she came into the public eye. For the last two years you can find LifeofLaura at an open mic, spending time with her husband and daughter, or writing poems for strangers. She has her LifeofLaura shows annually. She is a part of a professional writing group and loves the Sacramento poets.

Written on the Back of an STI Test Result

after "Girl, So Confusing" by Charli XCX (Lorde's verse)

At these depths, I'm a body / waving hi to these strangers

go on and go draw a bath / I got lesions to baptize

As for who is the father / I can't say and that's OK

"don't gift yourself all this grief" / is what a dear friend told me

 after he and my boyfriend / took turns ruffling my feathers

They went half on a bouquet / it's ok that I don't fly

we country boys, we make do / even when we are grounded

My thing for arm hair's intact / I guess that's how I got here

My boy, forgiveness is near / the love's been inconsistent

but body, it's now launching / even if someone's livid

I'll learn how to wrap presents / right here in this lit hallway

and I will see it again / see my outfit through windows

call the nurse by their first name / Google calendar notice

I know the bus routes by heart / God's strongest soldiers intact

Trust that my Virgin has seen / she is so omnipresent

Go on and go do your thing / just remember be safe babe ~

Oswaldo Vargas is a former farmworker and a 2021 recipient of the Undocupoets Fellowship. He has been anthologized in Nepantla: An Anthology Dedicated to Queer Poets of Color (Nightboat Books, 2018) and the forthcoming Here to Stay: Poetry & Prose from the Undocumented Diaspora(HarperCollins, 2024). His work can also be found in Huizache: The Magazine of a New America, The Common, The West Trade Review, and Narrative Magazine (among others). He lives and dreams in Sacramento, CA.

Tornado

Dear Tornado of Cat Hair in the bedroom:

Sweet kitty cuddles
on a cold winter night
are such a joy.

My anger at not
finding the flip flops
I like at target
melt away and dissolve
from the persistent drizzle
 of purrs.

But please,
Tornado of Cat Hair
that tears through
our bedroom in the
wake—

Don't become sentient.
We can't afford the pet insurance.

Sincerely,
 A Crazy Cat Mom

April Booth holds a Ph.D. in Physiology from University of California, Davis. She has recently started writing poetry again. A long time ago, she had one poem published in the San Joaquin Review while she was attending Fresno State. She currently lives in West Sacramento with her husband, two cats, three pigeons, and two tanks-worth of fishy friends.

Home Sweet Homeless

Harmless

That's what I tell the cops

This glass pipe

This acetylene torch

They aren't harming anyone but me.

They cops laugh

In uncomfortable boredom

As they

Drag me

Kicking and screaming

In my underwear

Out from underneath the burning I beams

Of the squatted warehouse

Myself

And my ten best

Imaginary friends

Live in

We all gather around a coffin

Perched in the middle of the floor

To discuss our new religion

Of living life to the fullest

By dying

Living

With radioactive rats who hunt for crumbs of meth

When they get bored of bullying

The anxiety ridden pit bulls who are

Wobbling from the stolen generator fumes

We all gather to burn the insulation off the copper wire

The building had electricity

And running water at one time

But we scrapped it all

The building is once again on fire

It's harmless

I assure the cops

No one in here

Besides the old man we

Wrapped up in carpet and left out

For the paramedics

Is really dying

My girlfriend

She goes where the dope goes

In clouds

 In sighs

 In happenstance

She

Happens to be just be

Standing there

By the coffin

Glaring

Inhaling the black smoke

In deep blonde

She stares

Into the eyes of

Whomever this week

Will make her

Syringe plunger dive bomb.

The roof is collapsing

The pit bull is panicking

She's really no help

She's looks like my mom

She falls asleep to me

Trying to convince her to leave

To get out

She steals from me

Bites my soft and tenders

Then flees

Runs

Home sweet homeless

Always

Back to him.

" He's got the good shit!! "

But it's harmless I tell the cops

Who simply ignore me

They break my pipe

Throw my stash into a puddle

Kick over the coffin

Like they did last week.

We've heard your story million

Times by now, son

Get some clothes on

That girl's been dead now

A number of years

" You gotta move on from here"

Home sweet homeless

Home sweet homeless

Home.

Anthony Xavier Jackson is member of GTFO Poetry collective whose work may be found in Tule Review 2023, The Word's Faire -The Feast Anthology, new words {press}, and BarBar-The Sweat Anthology. Anthony is a counselor, musician, producer and survivor of trauma who believes wholeheartedly in the healing power of words and music.

Water

Time slips past people

Without a second to spare

Like water hurrying off a hard surface

But not with us

No, with us time poured

And we stood still

The water in your laughter

Sank into the soil of my skin

Until something bloomed

The grass was never so green

Water in words we'd flow

We drank them like brilliant discoveries

Gulping gallons then gasping for air

An overflowing oasis after harsh heats

We return to the reservoir

Sipping from each other's cupped hands

A pair of poor parched things

For a few months

Everything was wet

We were spilling everywhere

And everything glistened

Catching every strand of light

Reflecting it back into time

Thanking it for the rainy season

Chio Saetern is a Sacramento poet and artist. Her love of poetry was born from healing and journaling. Her love of the poetry community came from the local open-mics hosted all over the Sacramento area. She is a co-founder of Sac Poets Society, a poetry writing and appreciation group that meets every other Thursday. People can find her amazing poetry on my instagram @chioetry .

My Poetry

I want my poetry to come from the petrichor drifting in through my car's cracked windows after a burst of rain showers down o the highway. I want my poetry to come from cloudy sunsets and power lines reflecting into puddles. I want my poetry to come from the lips of other poets who have walked such different live than mine, yet tenderly share this love of words we each hold close. I want my poetry to come from a heart so full it spills out into lines and stanzas written fervently in parked cars because this feeling just couldn't wait. Poetry will come from tears, oh it will always come from tears, from the passion of anger, and the wounds of betrayals. From friends and lovers that never lasted for forever. From giving up on the notion that much of anything is forever. But my poetry will also come from the laughter of my nephews, my dog's warm body as we bathe in sunshine together, and from the unconditional love that's cradled me my whole life. I will find poetry in all the first kisses I've yet to have. Listen to unwritten verses in the squelch of my boots as I walk on rain soaked pavement. I will wait patiently for poetry when she hides from me, and embrace her when she decides it's time to play again. I will be a poet, an ever changing notion.

Riah in the Sky is a queer Chicana poet just starting out in the Sacramento poetry scene. She has had a love of stories and writing for as long as she can remember. She first fell in love with poetry in sixth grade and immediately took to the form as a way to express the things she otherwise had only known to keep inside. This community has already given her so much, She's excited to give back to it through the poetry writing group She has co-founded called Sacramento Poets Society. Connecting with other writers to share in our craft together has brought a new, special kind of magic and inspiration into her life

no irony in occupied Palestine

I sit in the bath for what seems like hours
The water rushes from the faucet seeming endless
Yet it will sate no thirst nor extinguish flame
nor will any amount of it make anything clean again
Almost 38000 dead in Gaza
no irony in occupied Palestine
Ash rains on the rubble of apartment blocks and eateries,
Schools, the homes of widowers and orphans gone craters
As far as the eye can see
charred debris that could have been
Anyone
The streets are a knot with no cord,
Threatening to constrict
On dry throats
When
Eyes try to cry
the tears are salt
Nothing left to wash away the sorrow
the water rushes
 past me
I could leave it on forever
And It could never be enough

Jack Ballas has been writing and performing poetry in Sacramento for 16 years, and is known for his blues poetry. Jack has just released an ambient poetry album available at https://soundcloud.com/jackballaspoetry/sets/i-am-whole-1

People Pleasing

How to be unapologetic
When you're way too empathetic
The answer I should be seeking
but I'm way too busy
People Pleasing

Peace Keeping
A habit learned
from chaotic evenings
A sleeping dragon that restrains herself from action
Hibernating with reaction
Cuz confrontations are such a taxing transaction

Always feel like I gotta walk on my tippy toes
Unworthiness eating me up
Cuz it's the weight of the phrase of
"Am I doing enough?"
The pressures of standards constantly feeding me anxiety
Cuz im just seeking validation
Like taking medication
The balance between
 knowing your worth
and feeling like a curse
Or saying "I can be there"
But should I be there?
When all this does is
bring my energy level
Way down there

Pleasing everything but my psyche
Tryin' to breathe life into what makes me complete
Finding my place with
positivity
and trying to fuel my creativity

Cuz without an audience
Who will I ever be?

Luna King de Betancourt! Is a born and raised in Sacramento native that's been writing poetry since the 8th grade. She was involved in a writing program for youths, 916Ink, in high school. She now joins open mics around the city and hosts shows involved with SAC916.

I Put It On The Devil

How blissful it must be to believe in higher thing, like a Holy
Spirit, it would also mean that I believed there was a living devil
a supernatural evil, one more powerful than what you see in
everyday people, so of course we would be misled when sin
stretches his hand

like if my friend had a moment of weakness, allowing Lusy to be
his influence, I wouldn't love what he did, but I'll still have faith i
him, so I'll forgive... now if his shortcomings could be looked
over, because he wasn't in control, then shouldn't I forgive
myself and my darkest moments

Like I'm not hateful that's the influents of satan, I didn't betray
you it was the same noose that was around the neck of judas
when he souled Christ out for silver, I don't think violently it's jus
Lusy getting behind my eyelids and feeding me vivid imagery of
ending the ones that hurt me, hurting the ones that burn me with
the never fleeting flame of envy

. and I'm not trying to convert on anybody beliefs, but See, if I
had to accept that it was me that chose to sleep around, or
leave my kids and run out, or cussing at my spouse, I could
never raise my head again, I would probably die of shame if I
had to confess that

. I felt lust as a married men, instead of placing the blame on
satan, I could probably never love again just looking at the man
in the mirror I'd see a demon starin

Because there's no scapegoat to take the blame for the times i
was careless, and though I feel empty inside saying it out loud,
I'll say it one more time and then try to forget it, I believe in God
so I can take my sins and put it on the devil

No Last Name
Born and raised in Sacramento, I learned at a young age how music brings vibration to our lives. In pursuit of developing my connection to sound I have used piano compositions, music production, song writing and spoken word to tailor a series of reactions to life. My mission is to empower our community through art and service, keeping these stories of our communities alive is my goal as an artist.

Do Better.

Do better
who knew better
Born in a fucked up system
Forced to be a go getter
How the fuck am I
supposed to do better
when I have no one in my life
To teach me that being raped
wasn't for my own pleasure
(who new better)
I was trapped in my mind
living in this world completely blind
living in a fantasy
just to find out it's all lies
Growing up learning to despise
the inner child cries
because no one hears them
and no one gives a fuck about
the tears running down my eyes
Everyone on the sidelines
Waiting for my failure
Little did they know
That i'm a true trailblazer
Sleepless nights
up all night
fantasizing
I was born in another life
Forced into this world
on my own trying to find ways
to survive only to find out that
I was born with a target on my back
Just because the color of my skin and my eyes
I keep trying to wrap my mind around
The fact that I'm supposed to do better
But

How the fuck am I
supposed to do better
when I have no one in my life
To teach me that being raped
wasn't for my own pleasure
(who new better)
Do better
who knew better
Everyday I try to strive to do better
but I am locked into my mind
forced to prove better
Do better
who knew better
When i was
Doomed from the womb
I was forced to be a go getter

JJ.DIDIT is an up and coming Writer, Poet, Rapper and Podcast Host of Thursday Therapies. She has a great love for God, all music genres, art, freedom of expression, and rap/hip hop culture.

4/24/2024

My friends say we are all adults and,

That we should be able to communicate openly and honestly.

To be able to rest and understand and

respond to each with dignity and grace.

I couldn't agree more. In the depths of my soul and heart

I know their words are true. But when faced with my memories

the wheel begins to spin, and I remember most the adults

I grew up knowing did a lot more

yelling than talking.

Fighting more than loving.

So, when I show up at, your door at 10:16pm

I feel I've just about placed the seal, bargained all I

can on the deal for you to just let me in.

Fully Expecting you to raise your voice and ostracize me

for my choice to dare bring you an Arnold Palmer,

for me begging you to show me a sign you are listening.

But I've only been Praying for you to slow down time

and the cars on the road...just one second more. But if I'm
being honest,

it's this sacred floor that makes me uncertain. I'm not fighting D-
mans,

my family stays praying for me to G-Man, so you see man,

I'm certainly hurting because when I draw back the curtain

the light shines through and I can see all the anguish

I'm trying to vanquish is coming from within.

I wasn't taught to regret love, but

through the tribulations I've learned to regret sharing time and

breaking bread to see the leftovers snatched and hidden in

pantries

while my brothers are starving for a seat

and my sisters are starving themselves to feel beautiful.

I wasn't raised to be stingy. But it's one thing to respect

boundary

and fund borders—to patrol them to keep out unwanted energy

alienating any chance to make new friends. But I've said once,

and

I'll say it again…the only time love makes sense to me

is when my senses fail me, and it seems

my taste buds might not be too fucked because this bottle of

Seagrams

actually taste great with an Arnold Palmer.

But it also seems I can't find maintain balance or

find an equilibrium to speak without taking shit personally or

passing judgment.

Alexander Antonio Cortez aka AL is a Chicano poet, mosh pits enthusiast and tamale lover. He is also a co-founder of GTFO Poetry and His work has appeared in Fleas On The Dog Magazine and Tule Review.

PETS

Crazy the Cat, was he my pet

Or was I his

When he was 4

The vet said he may not have long

To live

But he returned to me

From the Edge of Death

My Brother late teased

"Crazy just needed to know you cared"

We had 13 more years together, Crazy and I

How many times did we

Fall asleep, his big body

Spooned by mine

His sweet cat cheek

Resting on my own

(and all the times he ran outside to greet me when I got home)

When we lived in the attic place

He befriended the Art store

Next door

Beneath the registers and office desks they made box beds

For crazy. I'd find him also in the aisles

"I'm looking for you!" he'd say

I hot a had neighbor, too

She and Crazy had a romance

One day Crazy walking me down the stairs

"Aww, sweet cat,"

Then, "hey where are you going?"

He'd walked around the building

I watched as he knocked

On Savannah's screen

A moment later

She greeted him "Crazy!"

He walked into her apartment

His tail up, entering as if

He owned the place

"What a smart cat, I said

Later on, Savannah shared

That if she was an animal. . .

"Look," she said

"The animal version of my name"

A picture of a cat who looked like crazy

"We spend hours together, I hope

That's okay," she said

"He's a smart cat, of course

It's okay. Thanks

For being so sweet with him."

Years later my wife – a lifetime ago –

She's now my ex-wife –

Teased me and sometimes

Said angrily, "are you married

To Crazy or to me"

He'd find ways to lay

Between us.

The Dear Cat

Nothing was harder

Than saying good-bye to crazy

I buried him in my

Sweater, one he loved,

And with a bouquet of flowers

The kind with white

Coloring on a purple background

And a packet of seeds

I've thought of the visitor

Phenomena

That often before one dies

They are visited by a

Loved one who has died

The visitor says, "your time is

Soon. I'll be there to greet you"

So I say if we can choose

Our visitor, then would

You be the one to greet

Me, Crazy.

Be my guide through

Death's Hallways, or is it a

Forest, or a pathway

To the Ocean

(and don't you want to see

Your Mom, too? And Chad, Ben, Lisa,

Brianna Lee, Stacy, Bart, Jo, June, Apple John. . .)

Crazy, I've known many

Who have died but you

Were the first one I

Hoped I would see again

Amen

Nate Beier writes in a diary everyday. From these pages flow his poetry and music. At some time his poems will be gathered into book form. Until then, please enjoy his music here: donsireno.bandcamp.com

For the Girl in the Tie Dye Shirt

Birds sing in the morning
and their chirps echo through the house.
The rising sun peaks in between rustling trees
and shines through the window.
A father gently shakes his daughter awake
and helps her pick out a blouse.
This is their morning routine,
if only they knew what they didn't know,
now.

She waves goodbye at the bus stop.
Her father waves back.
He smiles at the little girl in the tie dye shirt.
Green, pink, yellow, and blue,
making rings of color with a beautiful hue.

The colors minimizing in size as they get closer to the center,
almost like a target.
If only they knew the color red
would be forever stained on that tie dye shirt.

Children chatter, getting ready to put on costumes.

Paper planes and high pitched laughter
fly across the classroom.
The laughter stops at the sound of the door slamming shut.
A man in black with death in his hands,
enters,
given permission from this freedom land.

Bullets are flying now,
like bombs bursting in air.
Shells ricocheting off innocent skulls,
with no one in sight to defend these youthful souls.
A classroom once filled with dreams and promise,
now a battlefront for children to sacrifice their lives,
so that freedom to murder can thrive.

America, the beautiful, land of the free,
with little soldiers who couldn't flee.
Red stained shirts, pale, white bodies and blue lips,
lie below an American flag
and pictures of past leaders and warships.
Screams and wails from premature lungs
cannot drown the sound
of grown men
shouting from their indignant tongues.

Fighting for their right to bear arms.
God forbid you take away their right to kill with firearms.

Perhaps if they could see a 9-year-old boy drenched in more
blood than a man at war
lying dead on a classroom floor.

Or hear the sound of a little girls gasping, fading breath,
drowning, slowly, inching closer to death.
If they could see the fear in a child's eyes
as he comes to terms with his inevitable demise.

How can this be a topic of strife?
How can so many people not choose the side of life?
Would they still tell the little girl in the tie dye shirt she should
have run faster?
That the teachers should have prepared them better for
disaster?
That her friend should have found a better hiding spot?
No, these are not the things 9 year olds should have to be
taught.

As long as there is hate on this earth,
as long as politicians value guns over a child's worth,
as long as the devil has access to troubled souls,
as long as we believe that this is out of our control,
I'm afraid we will continue to bury more innocent lives,
for the sake of being a country that pretends to be pro life.

Please tell me we don't live in a world where children mean less
than guns.
Please tell me,
that something will be done.

Until then,
another day moves on.
The birds chirp but do not sing.
The sun rises but it does not shine.
A father wakes in his house,
but cannot handle the hurt,
if only he could see,
even just one more time,
his little girl in the tie dye shirt.

Lauren Helfer resides in Sacramento where she works as a Registered Nurse at a substance abuse facility. She finds science fascinating, but being a nurse over the years, she has learned that people are even more fascinating. She's been writing privately the majority of her life, but recently decided to step out of her comfort zone and share her work with the public. She loves to incorporate politics and psychology into her work and won't hesitate to write about loneliness, mental health, feminine rage, unrequited love, and of course, the joys and jitters of falling in love. In her free time, she will be seen playing tennis, booking flights for travel, and screaming songs by Chappell Roan or Taylor Swift in the car.

Untitled

I remember Granma used to take me to Toy's R Us on my birthday. She let me pick out any toy I wanted. She always drove a big four door Chevy Impala, which she handled like a champ. Although addled with arthritis in her early twenties she moved with grace. Appearing diminutive and frail, she was more than her body. Granma's love had no bounds. She taught me love and sharing. Granma didn't let her pain stop her from making us feel special.

You know how Granma's do, the good ones anyway. The pain was so bad in her joints she sought relief in various ointments and religions.

She was there the night I witnessed speaking in tongues, in that little living room surrounded by her Pentecostal congregation. Granma's faith brought her relief when nothing else would.

Although she was chronically frail, Granma's quick and abrupt passage in my thirteenth year stung hard. She was the first person I lost. I had no outlet for my frustration with the futility of life. Life is here and gone before you know it. Used to piss me off now I deal with it.

My Granma gave me the gift of family, faith and the optimism to move forward in pain. Life may not get better but it will change how we roll with the changes will affect our happiness. Enjoy your health and family while you have them, create the memories that will insulate you when times are trying. Granma taught me in the face of chronic pain that it's better to help others than wallow in self-misery. Live your life like it has an end.

Anthony Robles is a minimalist poet, exploiting the haiku and cinquain forms. Anthony is a contributor to the Sacramento Poetry Day curriculum, a charter member of GTFO, and a first time dog owner

Familiar

Today I woke up
Told myself I'm in love
With the man inside the mirror
And the black man I call brother
Apparently from a different mother

America feeding the lies
Kept between the world and me
Tried to tell us that we're strangers
That's the story of my life

I realize
I know this man already
I recognize
The pain in his eyes

Unification is the way
This is a hill I would die on
Remove the weight of the world
So you have a shoulder to cry on

There's power
In uplifting your brothers
That's why they rather see us
Killing each other

Should be healing ya mans
Don't punch down on others
Pull em up
With our healing hands

Black man
have you cried today
Have you killed your pride
And put your ego aside today
You don't have to be strong

All the time and do this alone
It's okay to be a drama king
Sometimes
go ahead and take your throne

I'm tired of seeing my niggas in the news
I mean my niggas in the noose
Murder scenes taped off
Making way for camera crews

Still haunted by the image
Of George Floyd being stepped on

Ride the light rail up the street
From where they murdered Stephon

Tyre was the big homie
He taught me how to kick flip
Saw RIPs
And hashtags next to his name
I almost lost it

I swear to god it feels like
In this world a black man can't have shit
I wanted to crash out over Tyre
Start a new revolution

But then again would my folks ride
Remember when Trayvon died
We was mad about the verdict
But still let Zimmerman slide

I said I'm tired of seeing my niggas in the news
I mean my niggas in the noose
Black men make sure before you tell a
Black man RIP
You tell a black man I love you

Incognito is a human from Sacramento who loves Sacramento.

Remembering the Good Times 2019

We haven't forgotten each other
Because we never deleted the photos
Phone shows on this day, with you, no worries

Remembering, Reminiscing
Getting in our feelings
I don't want it, you can keep it

I find that, without you, there's meaning
I'm the furthest thing from empty
Leave me alone, I'm so close to forgetting

Matthew Nazereno, AKA Niko Patron, grew up in Surprise, Arizona and has been living in Sacramento for 6 years. Of himself, he says: " Just a dude caught up in the mix."

The Assassin's Creed

A murder of crows on a cursed bloody morning with gales in the garbage and Spikes in the tyres. The place we called home's now a magnet for strangers with cannibal instincts. I told you to drive. Hear the choking of engines, a croak from the wire. They bulldozed the neighbours and set them on fire. And breakfast was bitter, no milk for the tea. Our cups left half empty cos we needed to flee. From the monsters at dawn . From the devils with wings. From the sirens , the smoke . Indiscriminate things. A wickedness spreading with mad viral eyes. A flesh flailing windmill .... Half alive.. It's mechanical, cynical , no hint of respect. For the land of the living , the realm of the dead. As the charcoal clouds hover to mask the decay. At the finishing line. Of the prize that we craved. Our noblest intentions left naked to rot in the pitiless pits time forgot. We forgot. They'll forget we existed and start it again. A million years . It will all end the same way. Way down Weighed down But still the sun rises...

Edward Ka-Spel is the lyricist and founder for the group Legendary Pink Dots. Edward's career spans 40 plus years of solo work and countless collaborations, including Tear Garden. Edward has graciously submitted these lyrics which will appear on the forthcoming Pink Dots album in 2025.Edward graciously agreed to share his lyrics with our small publication.

Cancer Poem

All we got was one toy and orange juice.
There was a days worth of ash in the toilet,
We hadn't been to church in a year.
The tile started falling off the wall.
When it hit the floor we'd stick it back in place.
Lots of construction workers contract pancreatic cancer
And leave with yellow skin.
When you go over some months, people get off goodbyes.
When your skin goes yellow, you know it's time to say goodbye
There's lots of widowers who hate the color yellow.
I hate the color yellow.
As well as wig shops, hospice, the Chicago Bulls,
Tucker Carlson's endorsement of Donald Trump,
And drives longer than an hour.
My aunt had no hair and hadn't drank vodka in years.
My mother tied a blue bandana around her scalp,
It fitted loosely and looked like a party hat.
I hugged my aunt with my right arm,
It wrapped all the way around her waist.
I then ate all the powdered doughnuts in her cupboard
And prayed in her garage until we drove home.

Dyson Smith is a Chicago born poet studying Statistics at the University of California, Davis. As a third year senior, he is currently working on Honors Thesis in Poetry titled "Tomboy Ballet," and his Honors Research Thesis on "Exposure To Gun Violence and Disparate Health Outcomes." Dyson serves as a Community-Coordinator and DJ at KDVS, a submissions reade for the literary magazine Open Ceilings, and a member of the UCD boxing club.

Penance

with the slant of rain
your sleeve drips
(Judas would never have his chance to repent.)
and your mouth claims there is nothing to search you for
yet there is room in the space of the six steps between us
made three and then one if i were to press my face to yours
it would return wet and red but never close enough
(Jesus had already died – and thus, in his final act, he gave the
very thing that he had tried to
protect: that was, himself in totality.)
can i know you utterly if there is room for doubt
(The silver he had pocketed for his deed held down his body.)
discomfort denied when i see it plainly
your shaking shoulders become all fingers
(As did the cloth he wore, as did the weight of his sin –)
reaching for a place that feels like honesty
(Until the noose would send him to a place where he might utter
the apology that would have
rather died on his lips than be spoken somewhere Jesus might
have heard it.)
even if it is spoken too late
[I will lay my head on your thigh and through the metal and rust I
will bleed, for that is where
you like me best.]

*Micah (he/they) is a queer, Californian poet. He has been
published in three journals: Beyond Queer Words, Basilinda,
and new words press.*

Smores

I hung my hammock in the woods,
just like you taught me.
Wrap around twice for good measure,
double knot to be sure,
and climb in with your fingers crossed for
luck.
The campfire is warm and I realize now,
I never asked how you like your s'mores.
That is, assuming you like s'mores.
Is it too late to ask if you like s'mores?

Allison Armstrong is an up-and-coming Sacramento poet who discovered her love for poetry after taking a poetry class at the Verge Center for the Arts. Affectionately known as "Grocery Outlet Gouda", Allison prides herself on writing cheap and cheesy poetry that captures authentic emotions through the situations of life.

The Book Burnings

The book burning began at 10pm that night.
It was attended by many members of the community,
a plumber, a file clerk, a surgeon, a restauranter
each holding their own copies of the vile condemned.
A sudden roar and shout of excitement as yellow-white flames
are ignited
The light reflected and mirrored in wide open eyes that were
somehow alive awake and dead at the
same time
The first book tossed on the flames struggled to take,
so they added clear liquid and the fire plumed,
creating a sound of awe and joy in the crowd—
soon the mob grew and grew and grew,
each gazing in own their self-righteous grievances…
I noticed a dark dirty grey alley cat staring at us from an orange-
rusty balcony,
an observer noticed only by me
the reflection of flames danced in the feline's eyes
offering a disquieting prophecy:
"This is a road you should not take," it said
"For this is the grotesque map which makes life unravel."
…

Nicholas Walker Herbert
Is a Sacramento-born local writer, artist, and professional
internationally produced playwright since 2001. He is a proud
member of Sac Poets Society, and resides in Tahoe Park with
his partner, his guinea-pig Goldie, and three kitties.

Electrifying Presence

I bathe in your electrifying presence as day breaks, the sun rising in the east, behind my gaze. I find that the best minds are naked, and I rest peacefully, howling for your delicate, delightfu delicious flower.

As I'm walking, I encounter a pond, where the water is so clear the mermaid swimming around in it could read my thoughts floating within the folds of my mind. I find myself giving you permission to cup my heart and hold it with the gentleness one does cradling a newborn baby. I imbibe your tender heart, naked and vulnerable, my devotion screaming and jumping off the precipice, full throttle, without worrying where it lands.

I'm surrounded by the sunlight of your radiant smile. Your splendid hair, with a mind of its own, rises like smoke from a chimney in the middle of winter. Our love is harmonious and no some superficial experiment.

Your gorgeous slender frame enchants me, bedazzles me, woos me, as if pixie dust has blown from your luscious and plump lips, which is quite an enchanting experience. There's a tenderness in desire as I kissed the air, my imagination lassoin your perfect image that's etched in the synapses of the humid caverns of my brain, seared into my memory for eternity.

In the grand scheme of things, absence from your presence ha only been momentary and well worth the pain, agony, and wait. The presence of your beauty, your mind, and your emotions in my life makes me tremble ever so slightly. When you fall asleep mid-sentence during our bedtime story telling of the day's events, I prick your lips with an ever tender kiss, whispering my wishes for blissful sleep. We must remember that in all our imperfections that we can become hypnotized by one another each morning when we arise from the previous night's slumber. The fizz from the champagne bubbles bit my tongue after my

toast to your motley collection of ideas of how we navigate our love life.
You say I'm your walking piece of art, but you are the muse.

Addy Sakler is 55 years old and a native of Cincinnati, Ohio. She has lived in many places, including two years in Northern Ireland. Sacramento has been her home since 2009, and creatively, she has found a family and a home in its vibrant, inclusive, and eclectic poetry community. She's a pierced and tattooed vagabond, consumed with wanderlust, writer, poet, photographer, painter, scuba diver, thinker, questioner, doubter, quirky, creative, atheist, voracious reader, audiophile, vinyl and book collector, breast cancer survivor, mental health advocate, autistic, female, Hez's other half, queer…

April

April was always kind to me
Full of romance and sisterhood
When my legs were freshly shaved
And my joints didn't hurt

I'd dance in meadows and swim in streams
Still gently waking
Mother Earth holding me within her embrace
A reminder that I am worthy

Your hands felt like sunshine
Trickles of gold and diamonds
Tracing down my back and across my cheeks
My heart becoming defrosted

Blooming dogwood smile
Turning my blood to honey
I am enamored
By your sweetness

But the leaves turn orange at some point
The bugs hide away
The mornings become crisp
And It's the return of the aching feeling I had almost forgotten

But still there you are
With your springtime love
That no matter the season
Never weathered

You are April incarnate
And I pray you stay this kind through winter

A self proclaimed "lover girl": Thea Miller is a Sacramento based poet. When she's not writing, she's diligently working on her Master's degree in Clinical Counseling, playing video games or listening to Nujabes. Her work dives into the spectrum of devotion, divinity, and determination in the face of misfortune.

She

From the moment I arrived on the planet,

Clean and pure.

Unsullied,

You preached from the pulpit.

Teachings of an angry Almighty

With fire and wrath in your hot iron eyes.

You taught fear of the creator,

"For the sake of our dirty souls!"

So I became scared.

As I grew, I watched my steps.

Small. Calculated. Timid.

Terrified to get too close to "the line".

Hold the iron rod, leading to the Tree of Eternal Life.

It burnt my hands in the golden sun that You created.

I feared the voices in the darkness.

Echoing screams of joy and delight.

Gasps of pleasure.

Moans of consensual desire.

So I became scrupulous.

But the silence, interspersed with murmuring prayers for

forgiveness,

Drifted to my virgin ears from ahead and behind.

We all cling as if to life itself.

So I became desperate.

Years pass like the blisters on my palms-

Playing back memories from the playground.

Screeches of innocent games

Alongside the most gentle "heathens".

Drawing attention to my heart,

Sutured in a million places.

So I became curious.

As I poke and prod at that most raw organ,

Open and exposed,

I hear the soft whispers of an omnipotent Mother.

"Love yourself as I love you."

So I became forgiving.

My being, filled with the sweetest euphoria.

She wraps her loving arms around me

Like the softest blanket.

Fresh from the dryer.

A scent of the sweetest flowers.

"I love you as you are."

So I became loved.

In this instance, I know

The true faces of Them and Her.

They are love, and so am I.

No matter who I choose to be.

I am she and she is me.

So I became love.

Meredith Gibbs is a poet from Wilton, CA. She began writing as a very young child, often competing in poetry and prose competitions for school-age children as encouraged by her mother, an elementary/middle school English teacher. After a long break, she has returned to writing thanks to the encouragement of one of her best friends, Chio Saetern. Her poetry explores themes such as healing from trauma, and finding her version of spirituality. This is interspersed with humorous winks at the absurdities of the world she grew up in, her past life as an actor/singer in Hollywood, and all things paranormal. In her spare time, she still loves to sing as often as possible, frequently performing as a featured vocalist in local churches and theatrical productions.

Race, Race

Aren't you tired of this Race, Race?
I am
To conform to a group of skin color
Our cultures deem that we remain separate
But when treaties and borders get crossed
I smell hate
It's the smell of bodies rotting, poverty, murder, cover ups and rape
Even desperation from the media to save face This is what we face
This Race, Race
So, I pulled away to see how the world truly operates
My lungs expanded
I took the purest form of air
My pupils dilated
My heart began to race
I felt alive for the first time
To be part of this thing that is bigger than our existence
To see pass the matrix
May we all wake up one by one

Does anybody know what year we changed our thoughts on food?
I'll wait..
One day it became the cool

People became more conscious
We cracked the code of a Rubik's cube
But existing now in this space with new eyes you better predict sad souls
They have become accustomed to the smell
They don't even smell hate
Usually I sit comfortably in their presence
But now I can't stomach the stitch of hate

They taught us about each other's race
Through music, social media, and news
But to keep it 100
This is the finest programming the world has ever seen
You were programmed not to like me

Whether it be my skin or sexuality
As I recited that line in the mirror it hit me
I was even programmed not to like me
But self-love set me free
From this downloading of a universal mindset
School and church followed order
Making sure morally you were addicted
Through the confirmation of propaganda
Putting Religion & Law In Holy Matrimony
Fuck these race rules
I'm a rebel devil, are you?

Even in the eye of my beholder I see beauty
But, no confirmation needed, we are living in Hell
It was easier the days I would be a bystander in my own community
Never speaking up, always head down
My apologies to the kids left unwatered
I ask everyone, have they experienced that?
And Yes, family counts
Going against your own people who don't see harm in their actions
Would they discard you for putting a mirror to their face?

How terrifying ?
I'm tired of this Race, Race
Appointed are the ones who elevate their communities and
educate
The cost you say?
Getting beat down until you must isolate
But if not you, then who?
We do it for the future of children
Keeping us humble
To be the adult I wish I had to run to
The reason I never liked conflict
It just fought against my souls' purpose
Aren't you tired of this Race Race?
I am

The Coldest Wynter is a Spoken Word Artist & Writer Straight Outta Philadelphia. Her journey in Cali has been an interesting one ! Still making strides to fuel her career and further her education in writing for film/television. To sum up who Wynter is " I Am Unwritten Poetry Pieces Put Together That Created A Masterpiece."

lady ellhorn

old girl doesn't suffer fools gladly

in the summer blaze

it is delightful to rest under her boughs,

it is delightful to wake among the fairies

her intoxicating redolence gentle as balm

knotted skin and cottony sinews

at dusk she stokes the fire, breath flows through her aeld bellow

beware she is not kindling

her scorch will bite you like a cobra

test your luck,

will the fae or the cyanide death get to you first?

Eliot Olson is a transsexual alchemist happy kitty bunny pony from Sacramento, ca.

The Good News

why does Desi

1 society still see

marriage as the ultimate symbol

of success? an unmarried 30-year-old

a problem to fix?

weddings are full of unsolicited remarks

from bas

2 and aunties. i brace myself

for the inevitable "hurry up and find a hubby,"

delivered with a not-so-playful nudge

phone calls with Neelam Foi

3

follow the same script

"we hope this will be the year

you finally give us the good news"

biodatas

4

look the same, too:

5'11, MBA, plays volleyball,

cares about preserving cultural values

yes, but has he lived? fucked up a few times?

it's funny that y'all still assume

after all this time

that i want to marry a man from the community

or get married at all...

rigid rules that make me wonder

whether y'all are living in another decade

altogether — more of your years spent in the

states yet the village mentality never left

Sonia married a white man

Dillon is gay

Rishi's dating a Filipina

each of them cast aside in shame

Disney and Bollywood lied

happily ever afters don't exist

"forever" is often an empty word

and a terrifying one at that

i can't stand that divorce is seen

as an unmentionable failure.

why talk about it when you can just pretend

the other person never existed?

mom and dad

don't even speak to each other anymore

dad's on the brink of divorce #2

so many eggshells you can no longer see the floor

spending money on

vacations they can barely afford

for that perfect facebook pic

instead of going to couple's therapy

always worrying

"what will everyone else think?"

instead of asking

"what do i really want?"

here's the good news:

i've learned that there's no other way

but to live by my own truth

even if that means doing exactly

what you don't want me to do

we appreciate the struggles and

sacrifices you've gone through in order

for us to be where we are today. but we

know what's best for us. times have changed.

it doesn't make us less indian

or less lovable

it just means we're opting out

of this cycle that's held so many back

charting a path forward

on our own terms and using our voices

when so many before us

were forced to stay silent

1 South Asian

2 Gujarati for "grandmothers"

3 My paternal aunt (names have been changed throughout for

anonymity reasons)

4 A résumé-like document sent around during the matchmaking

process

Brina Patel is a Sacramento-based writer whose work primarily covers mental health and South Asian culture. Her articles have been featured in a variety of outlets, including POPSUGAR,

Well+Good, Verywell Mind, and Wondermind. She also writes a Substack newsletter, The Tuesday Tapestry, which delves into a variety of topics — travel, mental health, creativity — through her perspectives as a first-generation Indian American. In her free time, Brina enjoys experimenting with poetry, blowing off steam on the dance floor, exploring new places near and far, getting lost in page-turning memoirs, and making memories with loved ones.

Flowers

I once was told
That the first time a man
Is gifted flowers
Is most often at his funeral.

Though grieving flowers are
Not born of gentle soils,
Neither is the soil from which
Men are grown.

We are taught to despise and avoid
All men who we do not know,
For who are they to be trusted?
Yet the point of it all is to not produce
Such bitter fruit in the first place.

To fear all sweetness but that of feminine nature,
Now that is a cruel test given to the minds of men.
The plague within our communities
Is the very notion, the deception, the horrendous lie,
That we are alone in our feelings, thoughts, and actions.
However, the more we breed connection,
The more clear it is that polar opposites,
Neither sinking nor swimming,

Neither ego convex nor concave in nature
Are the answers to our lack of love.

Rather, if we speak into each other's eyes, and feel our words
vibrate through our bodies,
We summon forth an intimacy incomparable
By frugal concepts designed to trap us in a quandary,
Limited by our own capacity to understand.

Instead of defining, defining, defining,
What our words mean and how they sound,
Just know their evolving nature,
And the intent behind them.

Instead of this, however, we seek to be misunderstood, rather
than allowing us to be seen.
Don't you get it?
You are known by others,
Because they know themselves.

We seek understanding by others, yet to know thyself is the
deepest understanding one could ask for.

We often are taught to seek what sets us apart rather than to
know we are one,
Even though when we move with the waves of others is when
we truly learn to surf.

So men achieve this, how?
The lone wolf,
The incel,
The patriarchal piece of shit,
Passing you by,
Telling you to smile-

Vindictive, though it seems,
They scream for their void to be filled,
And instead find a fist in their face,

As perhaps they should.

Think with their dick, don't they?
Treating their symptom without
Acknowledging their root cause:
their loneliness,
Engaged in a culture that teaches them
Pride instead of prowess

They equate softness with weakness,
Not knowing the lack thereof preys on their downfall.
To know thyself is to know the feminine,
The soft and passive,
The very flow itself.

Let us raise the empress back upon her throne,
Within ourselves,
And within our community.
For she is divine, yet unknown to many.

Let us meet again when the sun is near the east horizon,
In frigid mornings during spring
After seed is planted 'neath the soil,
May we ask who this next
harvest is intended for.

When time comes,
The difficult work is done-
to uproot, to pluck, to gather;
Even the ugliest fruits
May have a sweet aftertaste,
And may we gather the brightest flowers
For those who harbor fear to wear them in their hair
When they still have color in their cheeks.

Kelsey Rosenberg tends to consider herself a complex person, in many ways. She has struggled with Bipolar Disorder her whole life, and therefore, she has very intense emotions. She discovered poetry in adolescence, and has been writing ever since. Writing is intuitive to her. She chose this piece as a dedication to someone who spoke the first stanza to her once, who is now deceased by their own hand.

Becoming creation

So long as it's more important

to write than be a writer,

you will continue.

Whether the words are

a doubtful shout, whether

any eye ever recognizes.

Because to create is not

for the sake of being a creator, but

becoming creation.

Max West has written a lot of poetry. He is also interested in music, photography, arts and the outdoors. He blends poetry with original photography in works called Poegraphs, which can be found on Instagram @maxwellwestword. He released the album "Spoken Music" in 2019 with the group Maximum West, available on Bandcamp.His latest poetry book "A Poems" is available on Amazon, as well as his early novel, "Fourteen Months and Two Weeks Downtown." More words, links, etc. at: flasheslightning.blogspot.com▢

Waking Truth

I woke up today.
For the first time,
  finally,
    I woke up.
I can see the smiling sun
I can feel the whispering breeze
I can just finally
               actually
                be me.

Now I feel I should back track a little.
You are probably asking yourself what I mean. I mean we wake up every day. Every day is, well, just a day.
   Wrong

Every day is,
  every day was,
   a living nightmare.
I was not me
  Day in
  Day out
    simply put I was
      a shell.

I went through the motions
Did what was necessary.
Tried to be who everyone told me I was;
   That perfect little
         boy
   An obedient
         son
That-

   NO
no no no no
         NO

   They were wrong
      they were all wrong.

So when I say
   I woke up today.
It means simply
   I am finally that
         beautiful
            powerful
               magnificent
         WOMAN
      that everyone
failed to see

I was never the
      boy
   the world tried to tell me
      I was
I am finally who
   I was always meant to be.
                  I am finally
                        Me!

35-year-old Southern California native Blasé Van Splinter, was born and raised in Lancaster, CA. She acquired her Associates Degree in Liberal Arts and Sciences from Antelope Valley College. She currently resides in Sacramento. This trans poet's story is just getting started.

August

August please, be kind.
I beg you, Don't take any more friends of mine.
Too many loved ones have been buried in your late summer soil.
August, no more turmoil.
Please Don't take another life and leave me behind with all this strife.

August please, I don't want to fall in love again.
All I ask is, Don't offer me a heart to mend.
Let me avoid headache and heartbreak.
No more will there be smiles I have to fake.
August, you were suppose to be a month of celebration but instead I'm left grasping at old memories with desperation.
My broken heart sits still with anticipation; of finding peace.
Please allow me to have sweet release.

August please, this year you have a chance to be redeemed.
You're the last month left to enjoy summer so sweet before fall comes in to cut me deep.
August, I can allow your sun to dry my tears.
And the warm nights to calm my fears.
Please allow me to breathe and be at ease.

August please.
August, be kind.
August please, please don't leave me behind...

Bella tells us that while this year has been hard, she has taken to writing poetry instead of journaling in hopes it'll better her mental health! For her, it's been a lovely way to explore emotion, writing, expression and to connect with people! She lives in sac and loves all of the niche communities from drag, to local musicians to poets!

Ashes To Ashes

We don't care what the law says

Rebels we are

We say

But

A secret among us

All the same

The damage of fires

Made of ashes of their own

In a green spot

Reminders in the valleys around us

Of the worlds larger fires

The weight

Of those small containers

Seem all the heavier to us

Than

We let go of my parents ashes

From

Standing over the final resolution of my father's wishes

Years after their deaths

Those burning forests had kept us from this final destination

My father as a child

Swam in the water around us

My grandfather started this camp

On this no longer island we are on

Lowered water levels

The world ever changing

Even probably name the island

The camp

For distant rich kids from San Francisco

A even larger distance for the kids of 30s & 40s

Given the tech and roads of the time

That San Francisco

Would become the city of my birth

For my mom

A child refugee from World War Two

Her life long pain

Quitted

Does anyone remember

Or

Care about this

But

Us

Even if in this cycled down history

So many mysteries

Still

We may never know

That is life

Hopefully pass

This knowledge down

Feels so final

This act

We waited so long to do

As I imagine

It will always be

David Alexander Quinley is an multi award winning artist and in many types of art forms in 2d & 3d traditional, & digital art. Has finished several short films. Docs & Fiction . Also a political & arts activist . Has run for public office. And, won. Twice. Started many arts and political clubs at College Of Marin's @ Campuses in Kentfield & Novato, California. Showed for around decade at ceramics sculpture conference in Davis, Ca. Shown art throughout Marin County for decades, and also in San Francisco, McNeese Univ. (Lous.), Petaluma, Sacramento. Was 1st webmaster for COM school paper. Which he also wrote, photographed for. He has been concentrating on writing poetry, fiction, and doing photography, the last few years. Has made electronic music. Choreographed dances. Has curated many art shows

Pussy whipped

Can almost taste the shame
shared between our lips

I admit each smooch we share must feel like a Sunday morning
where a fiend gets his first hit

Gah damn
Already need another hit

Doctor doctor!

When will I get my prescription for this fix?

Another addiction disguised in soft thighs
Now this is the ultimate body high

Doctor doctor

I think we finally found a cure
Will this make everything alright?

Is it better than resting my head against
an oak tree huffing what comes at arms reach

Gazing at the sweet abyss
Now doesn't that cloud look like a rhino?

Nah that's a magpie
See that one there

That cloud right over there
resembles a man lost in the divine
All that he wants Is to call her mine

David Zepeda is a photographer born and raised in Oakland. After moving to Sacramento, he found a love for the art community and roamed around the city capturing concerts and intimate moments with friends.

Remember, Don't be an asshole.

Made in the USA
Las Vegas, NV
17 October 2024

97033700R00066